Dear Black Girl

WRITTEN BY ROZZANNE WALTERS
ILLUSTRATED BY JEVON FORRESTER

YOUR NAME TELLS YOUR STORY, WRITE IT.

Morning Sunshine!

Good Morning, Today is going to be a great day!

I am in control, I am going to make the best of today

My skin is glowing, my hair is shiny

I am the future, my dreams aren't tiny

I am loved, I am strong

I am beautiful looking like who I am

I am Able

I am brave, I am strong

I am powerful, No I'm not wrong

I can be anything that I want to be

A teacher, an athlete, the impossible, don't you believe?

I am black and that doesn't crack

I am the future and I'm not looking back

I am able

I am not confined

Because nothing is impossible in my mind

FRUIT PUNCH

MY BEAUTIFUL CHILD, YOU ARE JUST LIKE MOMMY
MOMMY'S SPIRIT, MOMMY'S HEART
MOMMY'S SOUL, YOU'RE MOMMY'S ART

YOU ARE NOT ONLY LIKE MOMMY
YOU ARE JUST LIKE DADDY TOO
DADDY'S STRENGTH, DADDY'S PRIDE
DADDY'S JOY, YOU'RE DADDY'S TRIBE

YOU ARE A MIXTURE OF OUR BEST
FULL OF FLAVOUR, FULL OF ZEST

YOU ARE DADDY'S SUGAR PLUM AND
MOMMY'S CHERRY BUNCH
A PERFECT MIX, OUR FRUIT PUNCH

Draw a picture of you

DEAR BLACK GIRL,

I am a Promise

My name is _____

I am _____ and _____

I enjoy _____

In the future I will become a

_____

because _____ can do anything she works hard to achieve

Love The Skin I'm in

I'm blessed with two shades in my skin

My beauty isn't just skin deep because most importantly

It comes from within

My spots are beautiful

They help to define who I am

No, I'm not sick, no it doesn't hurt

Yes, I'm just like you

One of God's gift to Earth

Write 5 things you love about yourself

_____

_____

_____

_____

_____

Adisa's CURLS

Adisa hated her curls. She wished her hair was straight and silky like her favorite princesses from her books and cartoons.

Adisa cries every time her mother combs her hair. "Mommy why can't you straighten my curls so I can have beautiful hair like Cinderella", she begged.

"No Adisa, I don't believe that you want to look like Cinderella or the other characters in your book. You want to be beautiful like you"

Adisa frowned, "No no no! I'll never win the Little Miss Princess Pageant if I don't have princess hair."

"ADISA DARLING," HER MOTHER SAID SOFTLY "YOU HAVE THE HAIR OF GREAT QUEENS." ADISA LOOKED A BIT CONFUSED, SHE MUMBLED, "BUT THE PRINCESSES IN MY BOOKS ARE SO PRETTY AND NONE OF THEM HAVE HAIR LIKE MINE"

ADISA'S MOM LOOKED AT HER AND SAID, "YOU ARE MY PRINCESS AND YOU ARE BEAUTIFUL JUST THE WAY YOU ARE" ADISA SMILED AND HER MOTHER CONTINUED, "YOU ARE NOT ANY OF THE GIRLS IN YOUR STORY BOOKS, THEIR STORY IS ALREADY WRITTEN FOR THEM. YOU HAVE THE POWER TO WRITE YOUR OWN STORY. WRITE IT WELL."

A FEW DAYS BEFORE THE PAGEANT ADISA'S MOM BROUGHT HER A CHILDREN'S MAGAZINE WITH CHILDREN ROCKING AMAZING HAIRSTYLES WITH THEIR NAPPY HAIR. ADISA WAS SO EXCITED SHE WANTED TO TRY OUT ALL THE STYLES IMMEDIATELY.

"WOW!" SHE EXCLAIMED, "THESE GIRLS ARE SO PRETTY AND THEY LOOK JUST LIKE ME, MOMMY LOOK AT THEIR HAIR, SO PRETTY!" ADISA WAS BURSTING WITH EXCITEMENT. "I KNOW PRINCESS, SEE WHAT I'VE BEEN TELLING YOU ALL ALONG, YOUR HAIR IS BEAUTIFUL" ADISA'S MOM SAID. ADISA WAS SO HAPPY, SHE SQUEALED, "THANK YOU MOMMY, I LOVE MY BOOK AND MY HAIR."

The night before the pageant, Adisa and her mom picked up the magazine and started going through the pages together. "Mommy, I'm glad you brought me this magazine," Adisa said smiling. "I'm sorry I didn't buy one earlier," her mother sighed. "I now understand why you didn't like your hair, it wasn't being represented at all in any of your books and so you didn't think that it was beautiful," Adisa's mom said regrettable.

Adisa's mom continued, "I promise to change that. From now on I'm going to buy more books, cartoons and dolls that represent your beauty." Adisa was so happy, as she was about to speak she saw the perfect hairstyle. "Mommy! This one! This one!" Adisa said almost shouting causing her mother to giggle. "Okay, let's see!" she said with almost as much excitement as Adisa.

Adisa mom started combing Adisa's curls. Adisa was not crying this time, she was not even a bit fussy. Adisa was excited to see her new hairstyle, she was so pleased.

When Adisa's hair was all done she hugged her book. Adisa was so happy. "Thank you mommy, I love my hairstyle," Adisa said happily. Her mother giggled and said, "You are most welcome my princess."

Adisa's mom was thrilled to see Adisa so happy about her hair. "Come on sweet cheeks, it's time to go to bed, you have a big day tomorrow" she said while pinching Adisa's cheeks.

While Adisa's mom was tucking her in bed she whispered to her, "No matter what happens tomorrow, you will always be my princess." Adisa smiled and said, "I just wanted to feel pretty, like the princess you always say I am." She paused then continued, "I don't need to win tomorrow for that, I already feel like a princess now," Adisa said with a smile.

Adisa's mom was so proud, tears began to fill her eyes. "You have always been beautiful and you will always be my princess," she said softly as she kissed Adisa's forehead and left the room.

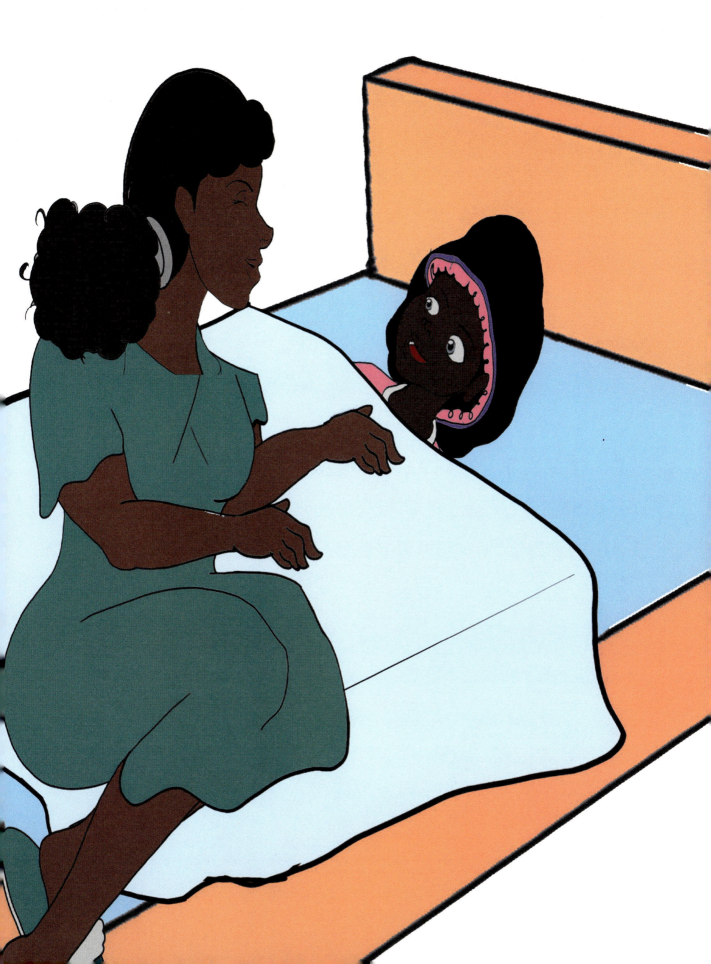

On the day of the pageant, Adisa looked absolutely gorgeous modeling on the stage. The audience was in complete amazement of Adisa. Adisa modelled with the biggest smile on her face, she was so confident.

In that moment Adisa knew that she had already won. She had already won in her heart because she loved every part of herself. She knew that she didn't need validation from a pageant to tell her who she is. She knew that she has the power to write her own story and she plans to write it well.

Editor's Note

If someone had told me five years ago "you are going to be an author of a children's book," I would have thanked them a million times for an awesome idea! I would have certainly included them in my notes now. But nobody hinted this to me, so here we are finally, half a decade later, with Dear Black Girl.

I absolutely love and adore children. Children can be compared to a blank canvas just waiting to be filled with love and light. Their innocence is unmatched. I sometimes envy their pristine outlook on life and how they see the world as a magical place. Regrettably, as they grow, that bright light gets dimmer and dimmer as they pass through interactions with different social mediums within their various societies.

In children's books, white or lighter skinned children are dominantly depicted. Moreover, black children are not usually represented as main characters in a children's book. On occasions when they are featured, they are often misrepresented, leaving our children void of an image to model. 'Dear Black Girl' tackles issues of representation that black girls from various groups in the black community face daily. Furthermore, the aim is to preserve and highlight the magic in black girls.

A few years ago I worked at a basic school with children between the ages of three and six years old. I have first-hand experience watching children learn negative stereotypes from their own peers. These children do not have an ideal outlook based on their storybooks and cartoons. Children with darker skin tones, shorter hair or a larger body type are usually bullied by exclusion and, in many cases, made fun of. Dear Black Girl aims to educate these children that every child is beautifully unique. Dear Black Girl also seeks to inspire and remind black girls of the accomplishments that similar girls that were once like them have attained. Black girls need to know that the future is theirs and that there are no limits to their black girl magic.

Made in the USA
Columbia, SC
03 May 2021